1

The Last Continent

When, in 1775, Captain James Cook completed the first circumnavigation of Antarctica, he wrote: "I make bold to declare that the world will derive no benefit from it."

Cook was responding to the centuries-old assumption that a vast continent with unimaginable riches filled the Southern Ocean. In the same year that the British explorer set forth on his most daring expedition, a Frenchman, Yves-Joseph de Kerguélen-Trémarec, stumbled on an archipelago, which he hastily assumed was "the central mass of the Antarctic continent" and no doubt rich in "wood, minerals, diamonds, rubies and precious stones and marble." In fact, he was still more than a thousand miles from Antarctica, and the islands he named South France, though in the same latitude in the Southern Hemisphere as Paris in the North, were bitter cold and barren.

Between then and now, Captain Cook's prophecy has essen-

The preparation and publication of this issue of the HEADLINE SERIES *was made possible in part by a grant from The Tinker Foundation.*

3

tially held true, although fortunes were made in Antarctica's surrounding seas and off-lying islands from slaughtering first seals, then whales, to the point of extinction. Recently there have again been high expectations that Antarctica will yield valuable resources. Attention has focused on its coastal waters teeming with krill and the probability that gas and oil lie on its shelves and hard minerals in its interior. As a result of the widened debate on the future of Antarctica, in the United Nations and elsewhere, opinion has become better informed and more realistic. Now there is a broader understanding that the existence of exploitable resources in Antarctica is merely assumed, not proven, and that if discovered, their extraction will prove difficult or impossible. Even in the case of krill, the high-protein, shrimp-like denizen of the Southern Ocean, there are great uncertainties about its economic value and the quantities that can safely be scooped from the sea.

Nevertheless, the attention focused on Antarctica has served to sharpen differences between those nations that have declared sovereignty over parts of Antarctica and those that have not; between those nations that have arbitrarily assumed responsibility for the administration of Antarctica and the smaller, more numerous nations that feel their exclusion is unjustified; and between those who believe that the exploration and ultimate exploitation of Antarctic resources are desirable or inevitable and those who, as scientists or environmentalists, hope that the continent can be protected forever as a world preserve open only to researchers.

Geography of a Cold Continent

Whereas the Arctic is an ocean bordered by huge landmasses, the "Ant-Arctic" is an ice-encased continent surrounded by a vast ocean. It is permanently locked in a mantle of ice two or even three miles thick and so heavy that it has crushed much of the land to below the level of the sea. Thus, if one could see beneath the snow and ice of western Antarctica, it would appear as an archipelago, while the larger eastern region would be an enormous slab of very old and stable rock. The greater part of the

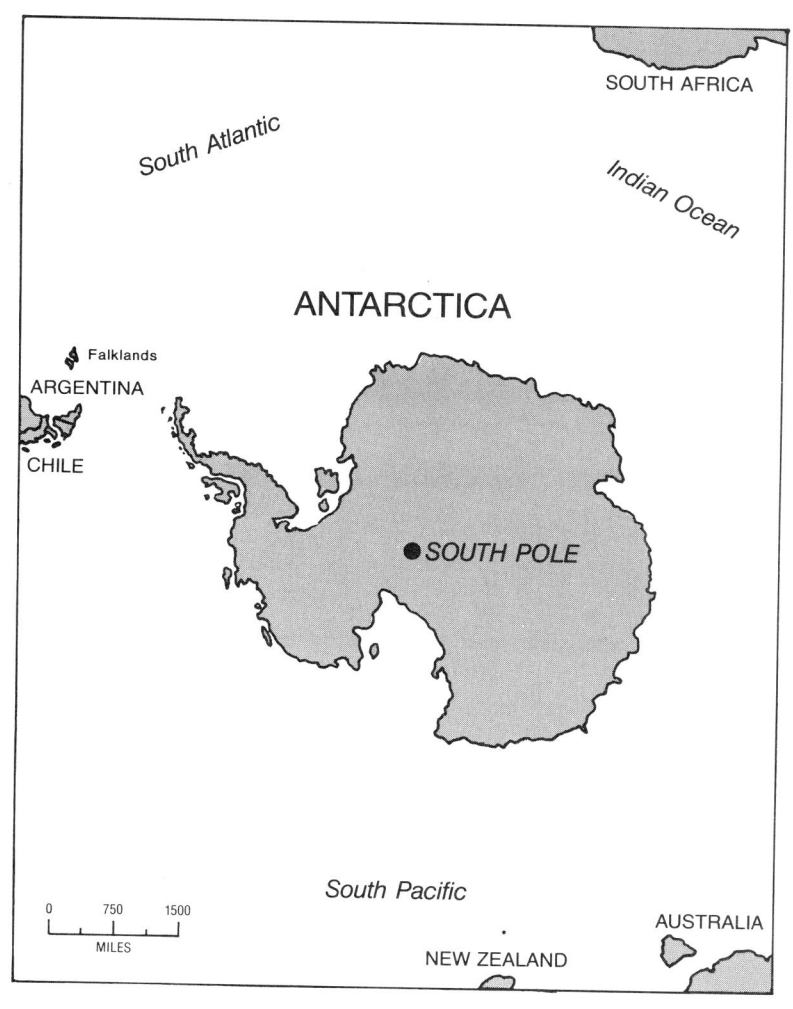

continent is a high, dry plateau where the temperature has been known to reach -127°F, and hurricane-force winds hurtle down glaciers blown into frozen waves of ice called sastrugi. Despite the awesome accumulation of compressed snow, representing some three fourths of the earth's fresh water, there is actually little precipitation except in the peninsula area, and the blinding

Discovery and Exploration

1772–75: James Cook circumnavigates Antarctica, does not claim to have seen the continent but probably did.

1784–1830: The heyday of seal hunters who strip breeding beaches, then move ever farther south to the continent until fur and elephant seals are virtually exterminated.

1820–21: The Briton Edward Bransfield, the Russian Fabian von Bellingshausen, and the American sealer Nathaniel Palmer are all in Antarctic waters at the same time, and each country claims its own as the discoverer of Antarctica. Another American, John Davis, goes ashore, probably the first to do so.

1838–41: Again three national expeditions explore the Antarctic coasts simultaneously: the Americans led by Charles Wilkes in a ramshackle flotilla; the French under J.S.C. Dumont D'Urville; and the British commanded by James Clark Ross, who discovers the sea and ice shelf that now bear his name.

1898: A Belgian expedition under Adrien de Gerlache sails down the west coast of the peninsula, discovers Antarctica's only fauna—mites and wingless flies—becomes icebound for 11 months, and very nearly perishes.

1898: A British expedition led by a Norwegian-born resident of Australia, Carsten Borchgrevink, winters over on the continent at Cape Adare at the western entrance to the Ross Sea.

---

blizzards that sting like sand are composed largely of snow moving from one place to another.

Antarctica represents 10 percent of the terrestrial world. Its boundaries are shrouded by glaciers 100 or more feet thick flowing out onto bays and gulfs, and by sea ice that expands and contracts with the season like a slowly beating pulse. The effect of all this ice is to reflect so much of the sun's light and heat back into space that the latitudes south of 60° are virtually uninhabitable, sustaining only the most rudimentary forms of terrestrial life. At comparable latitudes in the Northern Hemisphere are such thriving cities as Anchorage, Oslo, Helsinki, Leningrad and the ice-free port of Murmansk.

Antarctica is alone among the continents in having no close neighbor. The Southern Ocean that revolves around Antarctica is deep and broad and incomparably stormy. It is constricted only at the 600-mile-wide Drake Passage between the tips of South

of the Antarctic Continent

1901: Three coordinated expeditions sail for Antarctica. Erich von Drygalski leads a team of German scientists to the Indian Ocean sector where their ship is locked in ice and forced to winter over; a Swedish expedition under Otto Nordenskjöld enters the Weddell Sea to explore the east coast of the peninsula, by ill chance is split into three parties, loses its ship but miraculously survives; and a British expedition commanded by Robert Falcon Scott explores the Ross Ice Shelf and the mountains of Victoria Land from a base at McMurdo Sound where it spends two winters.

1907: Ernest Shackleton, with three companions, slogs to within 97 miles of the South Pole, while another team plants the British flag at the south magnetic pole.

1911: With total concentration and excellent planning, the Norwegian Roald Amundsen reaches the South Pole in December, more than a month ahead of Scott's ill-planned expedition that perishes on the return trip.

1914: In possibly the greatest of all Antarctic sagas, Shackleton fails heroically but tragically to cross the continent from the Weddell Sea to the Ross Sea.

1928: Richard E. Byrd leads the first of four American expeditions, based at Little America on the Ross Ice Shelf, using the airplane, the radio and tracked vehicles to explore vast areas, primarily in what is now Marie Byrd Land. The third and fourth expeditions bracket World War II.

America and the Antarctic Peninsula. In addition to the currents that flow both east and west around Antarctica, there are cold waters flowing northward. Where they meet warmer waters moving south—roughly at the 50th parallel of latitude—there occurs a rapid change not only in water temperature but in chemistry and biology as well. This undulating belt girdling the Southern Hemisphere is the Antarctic Convergence, which forms the invisible boundary of the largest marine ecosystem on earth. Because the convergence serves as a barrier to virtually all species except whales, the biological communities of the southern polar regions are quite distinct. They are also enormously productive: the richness of the sea is in sharp contrast to the biological poverty of the land. The nutrient-rich waters of the Southern Ocean sustain 20 species of whales and 8 species of seals, comprising one of the largest concentrations of mammals on earth, as well as 7 species of penguins with a total population of perhaps 75 million.

The Commonwealth of Science

From earliest times, scientific curiosity has drawn men (and recently women) to Antarctica, first because it was intolerable to be ignorant of any place on earth, later in the hope that this inhospitable continent would add to knowledge of our planet and our universe. It is true, of course, that the desire for fame and fortune and the hope of territorial conquest played a part in the discovery and exploration of Antarctica, and even today a complex of national interests serves to spur research. But whether scientific knowledge was the true objective or was used to obscure less-elevated aims, the 19th- and early 20th-century explorers of Antarctica demonstrated a remarkable commitment to science, often at the risk of their lives. The first winter journey in Antarctica (1911) by Edward A. Wilson and two companions, a uniquely hazardous venture conducted in total darkness, was for the purpose of finding unhatched penguin eggs. The failure of Robert Falcon Scott to return safely from the South Pole was due at least in part to the distraction of scientific work; among the very few possessions dragged by Scott and his party to the final camp where they perished were 37 pounds of rock specimens.

Every expedition from Captain Cook's onward included a number of scientists. The expeditions of the mid-19th century all sought to advance knowledge in the then emergent field of earth magnetism; and the Americans under Charles Wilkes returned with some 100,000 items—mineral, zoological and botanical—despite heavy losses of men and equipment. Virtually all the early explorers of this century preserved their scientific samples no matter how harrowing the conditions or how many lives were at risk. Ernest Shackleton, a nonscientist fired with ambition, was very nearly the first to reach the South Pole, but when he was forced to turn back, he brought with him pieces of coal, fossilized wood and plants, providing the first evidence that even the interior of Antarctica had once had a temperate climate.

The reason for emphasizing the role of science in the discovery and exploration of Antarctica is to gain a perspective on the present, when science is still the principal activity in Antarctica and knowledge its only export. Science is intimately linked with the heroic era of exploration, which plays a part in the thinking of those nations that have been most involved in this bleak and beautiful continent. Science is the thread that runs through the short history of Antarctica and ties it to the present.

The International Geophysical Year

In 1950 a group of American scientists conceived the idea that a major international polar research effort, with many participants and components carefully coordinated, would yield answers to important questions about Antarctica—for example, the thickness of the ice sheet and its effect on global weather and on the dynamics of the Southern Ocean. Multiple, simultaneous observations would also contribute to knowledge of auroras, cosmic rays and the ionosphere. Recent advances in science and technology, they believed, would make possible a quantum leap in our understanding of polar phenomena, if an adequate international effort was made.

What was originally suggested as the Third International Polar Year became the even larger, more complex International Geophysical Year (IGY), administered by a committee of the International Council of Scientific Unions (ICSU). Nonetheless there was strong emphasis on the poles, especially Antarctica. During the IGY, which ran for 18 months commencing July 1, 1957, 12 nations operated 60 stations in the Antarctic. All but one of these nations had had at least some experience in Antarctica in this century. The exception was the Soviet Union, which had shown no interest in the south polar region, except for whaling, since the circumnavigation of Fabian Bellingshausen in the early 19th century. But at the last moment the Soviets decided to participate. They made a spectacular entry, stunning the world with Sputnik as the IGY was getting under way. Though late getting started, the Soviets mounted a major effort in some of the most inhospitable parts of the continent.

Although the IGY was conceived and directed by scientists and yielded rich returns in knowledge, the operation inevitably became politicized. Given the complexity of the logistics and the high cost of conducting research in such a hostile climate, the involvement of governments was inescapable. In the case of the United States, the National Security Council decided that the U.S. effort would be second to none, the Defense Department insisted on providing more research stations (seven in all) than the scientists asked for, and the Seabees wrought miracles of construction, including a base at the South Pole for which 800 tons of matériel were flown in and dropped from the air. Other countries also determined the nature and level of their effort as much by their perception of national interest as by scientific judgment.

The Continuing Importance of Science

As the IGY came to a close, a fierce debate arose in Washington over who should plan and carry out a continuing scientific program in Antarctica. Some, especially in Congress, wanted to create an independent or quasi-governmental commission, named for Admiral Richard E. Byrd. Others were primarily concerned that the Defense Department and the Committee on Polar Research, both of which had played a preeminent role in the U.S. IGY program, should have continuing responsibilities. In the end, the White House chose the National Science Foundation (NSF), a post-World War II creation which had played a significant role in the IGY but was still seeking to establish its reputation. Logistic support was to be provided by the Navy. The significance of this decision is that emphasis was placed, and remains today, on pure research, largely unrelated to the search for resources. The United States Antarctic Research Program (within the Division of Polar Programs of the NSF) does not itself conduct research and does not even plan a coherent program of research. Rather, with the help of peer review, it chooses from among unsolicited submissions those projects it considers most worthy of support. This method is not without merit: within certain limits, it keeps the program flexible and the administrators objective. But it causes the program to be tilted toward academia (almost all projects are proposed and carried out by universities), and it frustrates those who want science to illuminate practical questions—for example, those involving natural resources. Also, it encourages both scientists and administrators, fighting for funds from Congress, to exaggerate the relevance and applicability of their research.

Another result of the decision in favor of the NSF is that the Defense Department gradually lost interest and expertise in Antarctica. The Navy was soon deprived of its own budget for Antarctic operations and all funds were channeled through the NSF, which simply buys the services it requires from the Navy and other Federal agencies, as well as a private management concern. Navy duty in Antarctica is considered undesirable, a dead end.

To this day, most of the IGY participants conduct research in Antarctica. Now there are more nations involved and additional disciplines, especially in biology, geology and marine sciences. Cooperation and coordination are fostered by SCAR (Scientific Committee on Antarctic Research), which is the descendant of the international committee that planned the IGY. It was established by the nongovernmental ICSU and is composed of delegates from designated scientific bodies in each of the countries involved in Antarctic research, plus representatives of eight scientific unions which comprise ICSU. A few other international organizations and agencies of the UN have standing with SCAR. Serving as a technical advisory body to the political management of Antarctica, SCAR makes recommendations to its member bodies and is responsive to requests from them for special studies.

Altogether, about three dozen scientific stations operate year-round. While the Soviet Union has increased the number of its permanent stations to seven (an eighth is rumored), those of the United States have been reduced to three. (A fourth has been given a reprieve of two years.) Nevertheless, the United States spent $111 million in fiscal year 1985 to sustain 99 research projects involving more than 300 scientists. Research in Antarctica is expensive: for every dollar devoted to science, about $9 must be devoted to logistics, broadly defined.

Science in Antarctica is directed not only toward a better understanding of the continent and its surrounding seas; it is an unequaled place to study global and extraterrestrial phenomena.

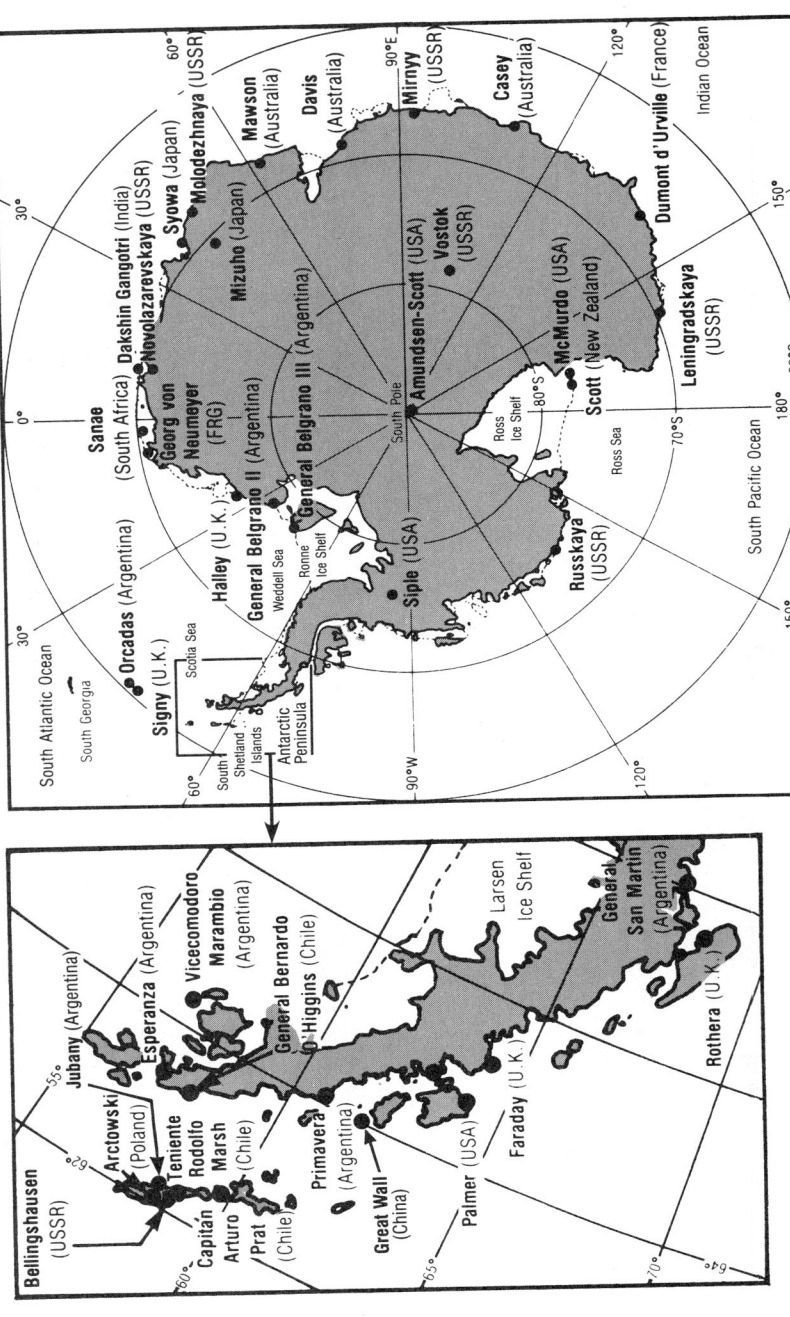

The high, dry polar plateau is an attic window on our solar system, a landing strip for meteors drawn in astonishing numbers by the magnetic maelstrom at the pole, and an exceptional laboratory for the study of upper atmosphere physics. Ice cores extracted from depths of more than 3,000 feet have allowed scientists to measure and analyze solar activity, climate and carbon dioxide over past millennia.

Although to the layman much of the research might seem esoteric, some has compelling relevance for the future of mankind. For example, if, as many scientists fear, the earth's atmosphere is warming, the critical place to monitor the phenomenon is Antarctica. A rise of a few degrees of global temperature caused by increased industrial pollutants in the atmosphere trapping reflected heat (the so-called greenhouse effect) might start a melting of polar ice that would have dire consequences for coastal cities, river deltas and other low-lying areas. There is even some evidence that a modest increase in air temperature at the pole might cause a part of the ice sheet to slide or "surge" into the sea. This would not only raise the sea level disastrously, but would greatly increase the Earth's albedo, or reflectivity, possibly offsetting the warming trend and causing a new glacial age.

Science is central to human involvement in Antarctica. Despite the omnipresence of politics hovering near, science has provided the rationale for almost every activity in Antarctica. It laid the basis for the political regime now governing the continent and informs all the coordinated actions taken by governments in respect to Antarctica. It establishes the criterion for admission to the inner circle of decisionmakers for Antarctica. It has provided what little is known about the region's resources, and if they are to be exploited without endangering the environment, scientists will have to show how it can be done. To a remarkable extent science has sublimated historic rivalries and nourished cooperation among nations. And for some time to come, scientific knowledge will remain Antarctica's principal resource.

Finally, scientific activity has been one of the principal ways that claimant states have substantiated their assertions of sovereignty in Antarctica, as well as a means for other nations to cast doubt on those claims.

Conflict over Territorial Claims

Of the 12 nations that participated in the IGY, 7 had previously proclaimed their sovereignty over pie-shaped segments of Antarctica. The claimant states were, and remain today, Argentina, Australia, Britain, Chile, France, New Zealand and Norway. Three of these—Britain, Chile and Argentina—have overlapping claims in the quadrant that faces South America and includes the Antarctic Peninsula. The claims of Australia and New Zealand, which were not independent at the time they were made, were initially asserted by Britain in their behalf. The five nations that have refrained from making any territorial claims, and recognized none, are Belgium, Japan, South Africa, the Soviet Union and the United States.

For some 30 years, the United States could not make up its mind whether or not to assert a claim. On the basis of early discoveries by American seafarers and the Wilkes expedition, and recent explorations by Admiral Byrd, Lincoln Ellsworth and others, the United States could make as strong a case as any nation. It repeatedly considered declaring sovereignty over the remaining unclaimed sector (less than 20 percent of the whole), where its primacy was unquestioned, or a much larger sector overlapping the claims of Australia, France and New Zealand. But in the end it always drew back: the unclaimed sector (Marie Byrd Land) was unapproachable from the sea; a larger claim would cause conflict with valued allies; asserting a claim might give the Soviet Union an excuse to do the same; and, perhaps most important, a claim might diminish the Americans' asserted right to move freely anywhere on the continent. The United States could hardly make a claim without recognizing the claims of others and endangering the principle of open access. Yet even today the United States defends its continued right to assert a claim in Antarctica.

There are many ways of asserting a territorial claim, but only one is unquestioned in international law: <u>effective occupation</u>. Though the term lacked accepted definition, it was assumed for decades that Antarctica's brutal climate made effective occupation impossible. Therefore the claimant nations resorted to a variety of

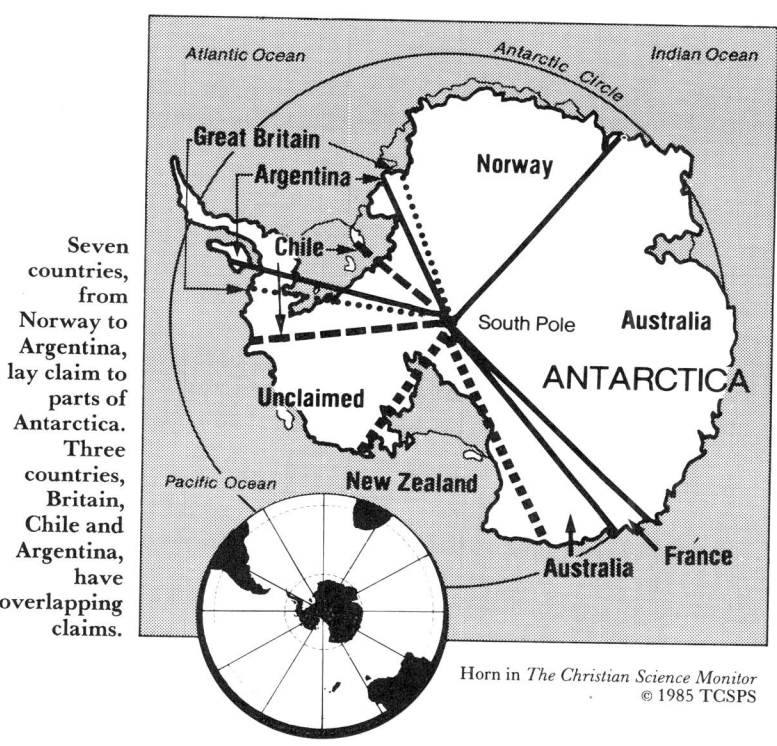

Seven countries, from Norway to Argentina, lay claim to parts of Antarctica. Three countries, Britain, Chile and Argentina, have overlapping claims.

Horn in *The Christian Science Monitor*
© 1985 TCSPS

means with greater or lesser legal recognition, and they continue to do so today. Britain emphasizes its preeminent part in discovery and exploration, while not quite denying Hugo Grotius' dictum that discovery does not itself grant title; it must be accompanied by "actual possession." Britain also stresses primacy: sovereignty over the peninsula and its off-shore islands was declared in 1908 without objection from other nations.

By contrast, Chile and Argentina, which asserted no formal claims until World War II, emphasize terms like contiguity, proximity and propinquity—each with varying degrees of relevance and legal acceptability. They even speak of geological affinity, the concept that the Antarctic Peninsula and Ellsworth Land, being structurally a continuation of the Andes, are natural

15

extensions of their countries. Such contentions may effectively contrast with the bases of Britain's claim, but they do not help to sort out territorial disagreements between Chile and Argentina.

The same is largely true when these countries assert primacy of a different sort. They declare that as heirs of Spain in the New World the peninsula area is theirs by <u>historical right</u>. They cite a succession of treaties, dating back as far as the 15th century, which in effect bequeathed to them all lands southward to the pole, even though the existence of Antarctica had not then been established. <u>Pan-American primacy</u> is another argument they muster, asserting that the Antarctic quadrant to their south is part of the Western Hemisphere and protected by the Monroe Doctrine and the "Rio Treaty" of 1947. The United States, out of deference to Britain, does not subscribe to this idea.

Another argument used by most of the claimant states is known as the <u>sector principle</u>. This was originally proposed as a means of defining territorial boundaries in the Arctic, by drawing meridian lines to the pole from the East/West boundaries of the nations bordering the Arctic Ocean. The idea works badly in the Antarctic, certainly for the Northern Hemisphere claimants, but for those in the South as well. Hence the idea was adapted so that meridian lines to the South Pole were drawn merely from the East/West limits of the Antarctic coastline alleged to have been explored by the claimant state. The word "alleged" is used because, for example, no Frenchman had ever been ashore on Adélie Land when that small sliver was claimed for France; and by no means had all of the vast coast of Australia's claim been explored by Australians or anyone else when sovereignty was declared by Britain. To this day, there is no consensus in international law on the validity of the sector principle.

A final method of affirming sovereignty is by <u>symbolic acts</u>. These have been used not only by the claimant states, but by nations wishing to keep their options open. The United States has probably raised more flags, deposited more brass plaques and buried more claim documents than any other nation, yet has refrained from a formal declaration of sovereignty. Other symbolic acts include setting up post offices at Antarctic stations and issuing special postage stamps, giving expedition leaders or their staffs civil appointments with real or imaginary duties, and heavily publicized visits by government ministers. The Soviet Union's establishment of scientific stations in virtually every segment of Antarctica—an extravagant measure that reflects political more than scientific interest—may also be seen as a symbolic act by a nonclaimant.

Effective occupation, the strongest basis for a claim, has become a reality. A number of scientific stations, including the United States' Amundsen-Scott base at the South Pole, have been occupied without interruption since the IGY. Moreover, at the tip of the peninsula, where the climate is relatively benign, Chile and Argentina both maintain year-round communities that include women and children performing a supremely patriotic and symbolic act.

In a sense all these arguments are irrelevant, all the symbolic acts are shadow play. The reason is not that the claimant nations are less than serious. Nor is it because the assertion or enlargement of any claim is prohibited, for the present, by treaty. The reason these matters are almost, if not quite, academic is because for the foreseeable future any serious effort to exercise sovereignty or, conversely, to adamantly reject a claim of sovereignty would destroy the Antarctic Treaty and a system of governance that has served the parties well. All the measures so far taken by the Antarctic Treaty Consultative Parties and all the efforts to negotiate new conventions pertaining to resources have had to avoid even the appearance of strengthening or weakening existing claims vis-à-vis one another.

None of this is intended to suggest that the claims issue is unimportant. The expectation that it would gradually fade away has not been fulfilled and it remains the most difficult aspect of every negotiation involving Antarctica, especially those having to do with resources. If national sovereignty in the continent appears less divisive today, it is because of the Antarctic Treaty.

2

The Antarctic Treaty

As the IGY drew to a close and it became apparent that the major powers would maintain a continuing presence in Antarctica, some difficult questions demanded answers. How could the friendly cooperation achieved by the IGY be sustained for the long haul? How could the issue of territorial claims be defused? Especially now that the Soviet Union was in Antarctica to stay, how could concerned nations ensure that the continent would remain free of military bases? In short, how could Antarctica be preserved as a zone of peace and a laboratory of science?

Some of these questions had been asked before, but in the late 1950s they arose with particular urgency. Antarctica was widely perceived to be of military/strategic importance, perhaps as a site for hidden submarine bases or the new intercontinental ballistic missiles. One of the principal motives for Norway's claim in Antarctica in 1939 had been to forestall an anticipated claim by Nazi Germany. In two wars Germany used Antarctic waters for surprise attacks on Allied shipping. Just before and after World War II, the United States mounted large Antarctic expeditions with undisguised military aspects. The overlapping claims of Britain, Chile and Argentina were perhaps the most dangerous source of friction, and in the early 1950s led to reciprocal harassment, destruction of installations, and in one case, shots fired in anger by Argentines trying to scare off an English party.

A decade earlier, in 1948, an effort had been made to internationalize Antarctica. At the time, when the Soviet-imposed Berlin blockade required the Allies to supply the city by air, East-West hostility had been close to the boiling point. The United States had invited the seven claimant nations to consult on the creation of a new regime, possibly taking the form of an eight-power trusteeship under the UN. The main objectives were to restrain the conflict over claims and keep the Soviet Union out of Antarctica. On both issues the proposal foundered. Argentina and Chile were especially hostile to anything that might appear to weaken their claims, and the Soviets, suddenly talking like old "Antarctica hands," declared that any regime established without their participation would be unlawful.

By 1958 the circumstances were quite different. The Soviet Union was pursuing a large-scale scientific program in Antarctica, second only to the United States. Also, the superpowers were as one in recognizing no territorial claims, refraining from asserting any claims, but reserving the right to do so. Most important, when the United States again suggested the need for some form of international agreement to ensure that Antarctica "shall be used only for peaceful purposes," it stated that this could be accomplished "without requiring any participating nation to renounce whatever basic historic rights it may have in Antarctica, or whatever claims of sovereignty it may have asserted." A treaty, if successfully negotiated, might specifically provide that existing claims would remain unaffected while the treaty was in force and that no new claims could be made. It was this proposal, contained in the invitation to a negotiating conference, that made the Antarctic Treaty possible. In June 1958, representatives of the 12 nations that had participated in the IGY assembled in Washington to prepare an agenda and reach agreement in principle on major points. So difficult were these preliminary negotiations that more than a year elapsed and more than 60 meetings were held before enough progress had been made to call the formal conference in Washington for October 15, 1959. A treaty was signed six weeks later, on December 1.

Provisions of the Treaty

From the outset there had been agreement on the central point. The preamble states that "it is in the interest of all mankind that Antarctica shall continue forever to be used exclusively for peaceful purposes and shall not become the scene or object of international discord." Its drafters were careful to add that "a treaty ensuring the use of Antarctica for peaceful purposes only and the continuance of international harmony in Antarctica will further the purposes and principles embodied in the Charter of the United Nations." The treaty specifically prohibits military bases, maneuvers and testing of weapons; bans nuclear explosions and the disposal of nuclear waste; and provides that, instead of international inspection machinery advocated by Britain and France, each participating country would have the right to send observers anywhere at any time to ensure that provisions of the treaty were being adhered to. Considering how troublesome the inspection issue has been in all disarmament talks with the Soviets, this was quite an achievement. And although the treaty does not provide for enforcement, it appears that all parties have faithfully observed its demilitarization provisions.

The negotiators had no difficulty agreeing to observe "freedom of scientific investigation . . . and cooperation" and to exchange information and scientists. But they labored long over the article on claims, finally adopting language that did not alter the principle previously agreed upon: the treaty would not in any way change the status quo on this issue. Nevertheless, territorial claims affected other aspects of the treaty adversely. For example, one of the weakest articles in the treaty and one that haunts heads of stations to this day has to do with jurisdiction. Supposing a crime was committed in Antarctica, who would be in charge? An unsatisfactory compromise was reached whereby scientists and officially designated observers, including their staffs, are under the jurisdiction of their own country, wherever they may be on the continent, while all others (primarily support personnel) fall under the jurisdiction of the state claiming sovereignty where the crime occurred. Fortunately, this untidy solution has never been put to a test. But imagine the potential for chaos if, say, a French tourist, arriving at the U.S. McMurdo Station in the New Zealand sector, were the victim of a serious crime committed by a person of unknown nationality aboard a Norwegian ship on a tour arranged by a British travel agency.

The membership provisions of the treaty are convoluted but, stripped of intricate verbiage, they pronounce that any nation may accede to the treaty, but only the 12 original signatories—the Consultative Parties—will make decisions. However, by unanimous vote, other nations that have demonstrated an interest in Antarctica "by conducting substantial scientific research activity there" may be elected Consultative Parties with the same rights and responsibilities. So far six nations have been added to the original twelve. Sixteen other nations have acceded (see page 62). While properly excluding the high seas, the treaty embraces the area south of 60° South Latitude, including ice shelves. The treaty urges peaceful settlement of disputes, but provides no machinery; fortunately none has so far been required.

Possibly the most distinctive and important provision of all is contained in Article IX. Although the treaty-makers refused to create any administrative body or secretariat—any formal organization at all—they did agree to continuing consultations "on matters of common interest pertaining to Antarctica, and formulating and considering, and recommending to their Governments, measures in furtherance of the principles and objectives of the Treaty. . . ." It is this provision that makes the Antarctic Treaty a living, breathing, operating system rather than a rigid document setting everything in stone. This capacity for change has permitted the treaty parties to cope with new problems as they arise and deal with difficult issues, including some originally avoided because they were too sensitive—such as the matter of resources.

The treaty does not say how often the parties should meet, but in practice consultations have generally been held at two-year intervals, plus special sessions for defined purposes.

The treaty has no terminal date, but after 30 years—that is, after June 1991—any of the Consultative Parties may request a review conference at which changes in the treaty can be made by simple majority. This provision has led some observers to expect that 1991 will be a critical year for the treaty and for the future of Antarctica—a moment when radical changes may be possible. But this is unlikely. For an oddity of this treaty provision is that modifications or amendments will not come into force until all the contracting parties have ratified them. If unanimity is not achieved within two years, the option of withdrawing from the treaty becomes available, but takes effect only after two more years. Thus the notion that the treaty can, within the decade, be altered by a simple majority is largely illusory. A decision so taken might destroy the treaty through the withdrawal of nations unable to live with the amendment. Because the Consultative Parties are much aware of this, it seems unlikely that any group would push through a change that lacked consensus. If this is true, then the situation in 1991 will not differ significantly from the present, when decisions of whatever kind under the treaty must be taken by consensus.

The treaty was almost universally praised when it was adopted in December 1959 and again when it came into force in June 1961 after ratification by all the original 12 signatory states. Because the Soviets had not set foot on Antarctica until the IGY, some powerful U.S. senators saw the treaty as a giveaway of American rights and "a completely unexpected bonanza" for the Soviet Union. But most observers considered the treaty a remarkable breakthrough in the cold war. Some of its strongest supporters, however, were disappointed that the treaty failed to settle the claims issue once and for all, provided no machinery for dispute settlement, and permitted decisions to be made only by consensus. These were seen as shortcomings that limited the utility of the treaty as a precedent for other "nonstate" areas, such as outer space.

Photo by Michael Parfit
A snow-block igloo which serves as a home away from home for scientists.

The Evolution of a System

Since the treaty was ratified, 13 consultative meetings have been held, the most recent one in October 1985 in Brussels. The parties have reached consensus on 163 "recommendations" on such topics as how and what information will be exchanged, cooperation with the UN and other international bodies, improvements in telecommunications, problems created by tourism, the designation of 44 historic monuments, and cooperation in logistics, transport, postal matters and emergencies. Since the delegates attend under instructions from their governments, these recommendations are, in effect, agreements, although they must subsequently be given formal approval.

By far the largest number of recommendations, as well as those of greatest substance, have dealt with protection of the Antarctic environment. The treaty members have designated 20 Specially Protected Areas and 21 Sites of Special Scientific Interest where access is limited; they have adopted a Code of Conduct for

Antarctic Expeditions and Station Activities and are soon to update it; they have urged detailed environmental assessment of any research or logistic activities likely to have a significant impact on the environment and considered SCAR recommendations on this subject in October; and in a variety of contexts, they have acknowledged their obligation to protect the Antarctic environment "in the interest of all mankind."

The treaty was only three years old when the Consultative Parties adopted the Agreed Measures for the Conservation of Antarctic Fauna and Flora. These measures provide that animals and plants cannot be taken from the Antarctic except by permit and as necessary for scientific research and education; offer special protection for certain species and certain areas; designate activities that are harmful to birds or seals; obligate governments to do everything possible to reduce pollution of coastal waters; and prohibit the introduction of animals and plants not indigenous to the Antarctic, except under license. (These permits and licenses are issued by each Consultative Party to its own nationals in accordance with domestic legislation.) In 1972, the Convention for the Conservation of Antarctic Seals was adopted, though formally it was negotiated outside the treaty structure. There is presently no sealing in Antarctica.

This record of concern for the Antarctic environment does not suggest, as is sometimes charged, that the Consultative Parties have behaved irresponsibly or selfishly or in disregard of the larger interests of humanity. Agreements on paper do not, of course, guarantee adherence, and more could be done—especially to enlarge and ensure the permanence of protected areas, and to protect more resolutely the environment around coastal stations. As elsewhere, regulations are often better than compliance. But on balance, the environmental policies and practices adopted by the treaty powers are not easily faulted.

3

The Resources of Antarctica

The failure of the Antarctic Treaty to deal with resources was not an oversight. The issue was simply too intricately entwined with the question of territorial claims to be manageable. And the development of Antarctic resources seemed sufficiently remote to allow the matter to be ignored for a time. Then as the decade of the 1970s progressed, the Consultative Parties recognized that they must grasp the nettle.

The Marine Living Resources Convention

Two circumstances tended to focus attention on the resources of the Southern Ocean. First was the recognition that most of the world's fisheries were being taxed to the limit or beyond; the harvest of many species was declining. Second was the recognition that the Convention on the Law of the Sea, which was nearing adoption after years of negotiation, would effectively exclude long-distance fishing nations from coastal waters they had long exploited. The pressure on the world's last great undeveloped fishery—the Southern Ocean—might become severe. Rather than wait until the fishery was at risk, the Antarctic Treaty nations sought to create a management plan <u>before</u> the target resource could be overexploited.

The target species is krill, the principal food of whales and other marine creatures in the Southern Ocean. A decade ago there were inordinately high expectations that this astonishingly abundant crustacean, rich in protein and minerals, would soon become a major source of food for man and domestic animals. Despite half a century of research, hard facts about krill are lacking. No one knows how much krill there is (estimates range from 300 million to 6 billion metric tons), how rapidly it reproduces or how much is consumed by natural predators—not only whales, but seals, penguins, squid, winged birds and finfish. Above all, no one knows how much krill may safely be taken from the Southern Ocean without seriously upsetting the ecosystem and its marine life that is uniquely dependent on krill. For nearly a decade a broad international effort has been under way to obtain improved data on these and related questions. Known by its acronym BIOMASS (Biological Investigations of Marine Antarctic Systems and Stocks), it officially concludes in 1986 unless extended.

One of the characteristics of krill that makes it commercially attractive is its habit of swimming in large swarms of high density. Shoals of up to 10 million metric tons of krill have been discovered by acoustical means, and trawlers have caught as much as 35 tons in a few minutes. It is this heavy concentration of krill that makes life for baleen whales possible. Without it, the world's largest mammals could hardly survive on one of the smallest of marine creatures. Therefore, in developing krill as a commercial resource, the greatest caution must be exercised.

Recognizing this, the Antarctic Treaty nations, meeting in London in 1977, decided there was need for "a definitive regime" for the Southern Ocean. Difficult and time-consuming negotiations began. Because the agreements sought would cover the high seas as well as Antarctic coastal zones, the negotiations could not legitimately be conducted within the framework of the treaty system. To get around this problem, the Consultative Parties developed a quite deceptive procedure whereby they made every decision but sought to give the appearance of involving all nations

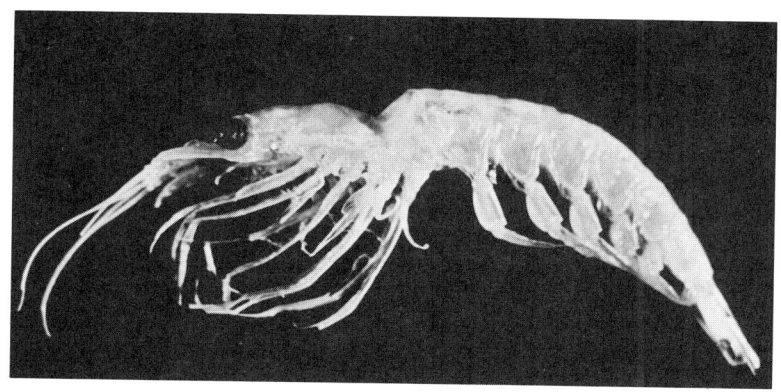

National Science Foundation photo

Antarctic krill, a crustacean just over two inches long, is the principal food of the great whales.

that fished the Southern Ocean or conducted research there; they then presented the result on a take-it-or-leave-it basis. Although the agreements reached were, in general, praiseworthy, the arbitrary method of obtaining them was an unnecessary irritation to the Third World.

The Convention on the Conservation of Antarctic Marine Living Resources, to which any interested state may adhere, was adopted in May 1980 at Canberra, Australia, and came into force in April 1982. The final document is a triumph of calculated ambiguity, of ingenious obfuscation required to bridge the differences between claimant and nonclaimant states, but the substance of the agreement is a modest breakthrough. The convention is distinctive if not unique in treating the Antarctic marine ecosystem as a single management area, where conservation principles reflect concern for all species and their relationships. It defines conservation to include "rational use," but then prescribes fairly rigorous guidelines for the harvesting of any species. It does not itself ensure optimal protection of the Southern Ocean, but is essentially a statement of principles which must be given substance by a commission representing all the Consultative Parties, plus East Germany, the European Economic Community, and other adhering states that fish or conduct marine research in

Antarctic waters. An oddity of this group is that a majority conduct no commercial fishing in the Southern Ocean and are primarily interested in conservation. Fishing conventions are normally negotiated by the fishing nations engaged in the area; never before had a majority of parties to a negotiation been primarily concerned with something other than commerical fishing. Perhaps for this reason, the convention contains an escape clause. After a decision has been reached, any participating nation may ignore it. Where decisions are made by consensus, this may not be as serious a shortcoming as it appears. But there are other weaknesses. For example, observers and inspectors called for in the convention "shall remain subject to the jurisdiction of the Contracting Party of which they are nationals." This means, in effect, that each nation is responsible for its own compliance.

On the more positive side, the convention requires that the commission publish data on which its conservation measures are based as well as the reports of its scientific committee. Further, "any activity contrary to the objective of this Convention" must be reported to the commission for further dissemination. The commission and the scientific committee now meet annually during August and September at the convention's new headquarters in Hobart, Tasmania, Australia.

A decade ago, conservationists feared that overfishing of krill might do irreparable damage before an effective agreement could be put in place. This concern turned out to be unfounded because the harvesting of krill increased much more slowly than had been anticipated. Krill proved difficult to catch economically; to process with the necessary speed; to shell efficiently; and to market. Though krill was made available in several countries as whole tail meats (frozen, canned or dried) and as mince, paste, powder and protein concentrate— each in a variety of consumer products— there was no rush to buy. Krill has been used experimentally as an animal feed supplement and in pet food, but it is expensive. The real economics of krill remain unknown, because commercial fishing has not yet developed; so far governments have done the fishing or have subsidized others. Only the Soviet Union has harvested a significant amount of krill—about half a million tons in 1982—and the total catch by all nations had fallen to a mere 230,000 tons in 1983, the last year for which figures are available. Nevertheless, the Antarctic marine ecosystem has not escaped unscathed: partly to offset the cost of experimental fishing for krill, species of finfish, which reproduce very slowly in the frigid waters of the Southern Ocean, have been decimated.

Negotiating a Minerals Regime

When the possibility emerged that an enduring shortage of oil might spur the exploration and exploitation of oil in Antarctica, the treaty powers began discussing the need for a minerals regime that would cover mining of hard minerals on the continent as well as offshore oil and gas. After 10 years of talk and six formal negotiating sessions, a minerals regime is not yet in place, but may be near. Originally, the Consultative Parties had hoped to conclude a treaty while the international community was still preoccupied with the Conference on the Law of the Sea. Since the global shortage of petroleum has temporarily evaporated, this delay is not a serious matter. The seventh negotiating session was held in Paris in late September 1985, and unless there are last-minute hitches, a minerals convention is likely to be completed in a year or two.

It will not be a detailed blueprint, but a statement of principles and objectives and a framework for the specific decisions yet to be made to regulate minerals activities. As with the Antarctic Treaty, decisionmaking will probably be confined to the Consultative Parties, but the regime will be nondiscriminatory in that any nation may participate in exploration and exploitation as long as it is bound by the basic provisions of the Antarctic Treaty and satisfies the requirements of the regime. The convention that finally emerges will almost surely provide for a cautious, step-by-step approach to resource development ensuring reasonable protection of the environment. Unlike the marine living resources convention, which permits activities not specifically restrained, mineral resource activities will be prohibited unless specifically authorized. Moreover, there will be a provision for the suspension, modification or cancellation of authorization if there is a failure to comply with the rules or if new and unforeseen risks to the environment should arise.

To avoid some intractable aspects of the claims issue, negotiators have focused on the institutions of the regime, their composition and the method by which they will make decisions. There will be a central body or commission with authority over the whole area; an advisory committee providing scientific, technical and environmental counsel; a secretariat; and possibly a number of "regulatory committees," where the detailed rules governing specific mining projects will be negotiated. This last institution, which will operate with respect to a defined geographical area, is designed to accommodate differing positions on claims. The exact composition of these committees is still being negotiated, but each will include representatives of the state wishing to undertake mineral resource activities in a specified area and of the state (or states) claiming sovereignty in that area.

Unlike krill, oil and other minerals are only assumed to exist in exploitable quantities. The treaty nations agreed that ground rules for resource development should be laid down <u>before</u> discoveries could set off an uncontrolled rush that might have serious environmental and political consequences. They have agreed to a moratorium on any kind of prospecting that could disturb the ecology of the Southern Ocean. Unfortunately, because the treaty nations acted with what some saw as admirable foresight and others saw as premature haste, many countries unfamiliar with Antarctica got the impression that vast mineral wealth was known to exist there and would soon be exploited. It is now more widely understood that the riches of Antarctica are highly speculative. Only very large deposits will ever seem attractive, and even if they are discovered, the economic and technological problems will be intimidating.

What are the prospects? There are three reasons for believing significant mineral deposits may be found. First is the simple fact that all other continents have exploitable minerals, and Antarctica is unlikely to be an exception. Second, scientists are aware of thick sedimentary beds, especially in the Ross, Amundsen and Bellingshausen seas, suggesting the likelihood of oil and gas deposits; and recently the West German research ship *Polarstern* found "unambiguous" evidence of oil deposits in the Bransfield Strait off the tip of the Antarctic Peninsula. Also, scientists have found large deposits of coal and iron and what they call "occurrences" of more-valuable minerals—that is, they exist and may or may not be economically significant. Third, the study of plate tectonics (movement of segments of Earth's crust) and the theory of continental drift not only lead scientists to believe that large mineral deposits are present, but also indicate where they may be found.

Gondwanaland

It is now almost universally accepted that Antarctica was once part of a supercontinent, Gondwanaland, which 200 million years ago began to break up into its constituent parts: the Indian peninsula, Africa (including Madagascar), South America and Australia/New Zealand, each drifting over the interior mantle of the earth to its present position on the globe. By reconstructing the way these continents once tucked into each other and noting the similarity of geological structures extending from one to another, scientists have determined with reasonable presumption of accuracy that particular minerals will be found in particular places in Antarctica. For example, the Dufek Massif, inland from the head of the Weddell Sea, once lay adjacent to South Africa's Bushveld complex, the largest and richest mineral region in the world, and may therefore be expected to contain similar mineral deposits. Or again, expectation that oil will be found in the Ross Sea is based in part on its proximity 50 million years ago to the rich Gippsland Basin off the southeastern tip of Australia.

Even if the presence of oil is confirmed, there is no certainty that it will ever be extracted. The conditions are uniquely hazardous. The weather is brutal to man and equipment. The winter nights are long. Icebergs as big as Rhode Island will endanger drill ships and scour the sea bottom at depths of more than a thousand feet. Almost every circumstance will add enormously to the costs of exploitation: the vast distances to refineries and markets; the exceptional depth of the continental shelves; the

The Adélie penguin rookery at Cape Bird, Ross Island

U.S. Navy photo by Howard Weinger

shortness of the navigable season (about 90 days); the need for icebreakers and reinforced hulls on all vessels used; the high costs of storage, staffing, equipment maintenance, docking facilities and shore installations. Only if there is a global oil shortage far more severe than any yet experienced will there be any likelihood of extracting oil from Antarctica; even then, the development of oil sands and oil shale will probably be cheaper. Exploitation of Antarctic oil would presumably require a variety of new technologies, such as submersible pumps buried in valleys of the seabed and flexible, submarine storage tanks. And it would probably require a political decision rather than a purely economic one; that is, a country like Japan, which is totally dependent on foreign oil, might decide that the advantages of a secure source would more than offset uneconomic costs.

The consequences of oil spills in the Antarctic environment are essentially unknown. Though probably not as serious as many ecologists declare, the danger cannot be lightly dismissed. One of the agreed purposes of a minerals regime is to protect the environment by moving in cautious and well-defined stages from preliminary prospecting to the actual pumping of oil.

The exploitation of hard minerals is even more remote; indeed it is almost impossible to conceive the combination of circumstances that would make it economical to wrest deeply buried metals from Antarctica's harsh environment. There is no shortage of iron and coal in the world. Even if rich deposits of gold, platinum, chromium, vanadium, cobalt and manganese are found in the Dufek Massif, they will be prohibitively costly to mine, smelt and transport. Processing, housing, everything would have to be underground, and large amounts of nuclear energy would be needed to power the machinery, heat the furnaces and melt ice and snow to provide the quantities of water needed for processing. The burden on the immediate environment would be immense, but an even more critical deterrent is that, in today's market, each dollar's worth of refined metal obtained would cost at least $10 to extract.

There is a further reason for believing that the resources of Antarctica may never be exploited—or that attention may shift to other resources, such as water and tourism. The technological revolution has moved to a new stage that may make Antarctic krill and minerals irrelevant. Biotechnology may provide new sources of food, and materials substitution may radically alter our evaluation of mineral resources.

For all these reasons, the notion that the mineral resources of Antarctica are soon to provide a bonanza for the treaty powers is far off the mark. Yet the remoteness or improbability of successful exploitation is not a reason to postpone setting ground rules and clarifying the legitimate interests of the international community. But even if minerals are ultimately extracted from Antarctica, revenues of any consequence are even more distant. Initially, any return from licenses, taxes or royalties will probably be devoted to further research and environmental protection.

Other Resources of Antarctica

Although the living resources of the Southern Ocean, notably krill and minerals, primarily oil and gas, have received the lion's share of attention, there are other possibilities that have long been discussed. Some of them seem less promising than they once did, while others may be anticipated with little enthusiasm.

Tourism has not developed as rapidly as many expected, but it may be the chief threat to the Antarctic environment as well as a potentially significant source of revenue. Today tourism is confined largely to a few cruise ships, sailing from ports in southern Chile and Argentina, and stopping to visit scientific stations on the Antarctic Peninsula. They are already a nuisance to the scientists working there, and any considerable increase in tourists would become a serious distraction and an imposition on those engaged in serious work. More ships would mean more pollution, and while tourists now are well briefed on protecting the Antarctic environment, larger numbers would likely increase exponentially the impact on the coastal ecology.

During the 1970s, Air New Zealand and Qantas frequently flew one-day excursions over Antarctica. In 1979 a DC-10, piloted by an inexperienced New Zealand crew, flying low in poor visibility so as to give the passengers a view, plunged into

Mt. Erebus, an active volcano not far from U.S. and New Zealand stations, killing all 257 people aboard. For the tourists in summer dress, without emergency gear, instant death was probably a mercy; and certainly a mercy for those working on the ice who might have been called upon to conduct rescue operations in foul weather. Since then tourist overflights have become infrequent and most come from South America. If tourism in Antarctica is to grow significantly—and many hope it won't—altogether new measures will be needed to protect the environment, set rational limits to the risks, and provide machinery for dealing with emergencies. This will prove difficult to accomplish precisely because the Consultative Parties are so reluctant to do anything that might be interpreted as a restraint on open access to Antarctica. However, they have already recommended that scientific stations refuse to accept visits from tour ships.

Icebergs as a source of fresh water for parched lands have been the subject of speculation and research, but so far the economic and technological problems of transporting enormous icebergs over vast distances have proved insurmountable. The gigantic icebergs that regularly break away from the ice shelves and glacier tongues of Antarctica often travel considerable distances northward, driven by winds and currents. The original idea was that by giving them a small nudge, perhaps by large sea-going tugs, they could be directed to the arid areas of, say, northern Chile or western Australia. But then more grandiose plans developed to cloak the icebergs in protective wrappings and tow them into the Northern Hemisphere. A Saudi prince spent millions of dollars to develop the technology and for a time there was some optimism that he might succeed. But it soon became apparent that no way had been devised to transport an iceberg across the equator and end up with anything but an empty tow rope.

Nevertheless, when it is considered that Antarctica holds about three fourths of the earth's fresh water, an increasingly critical resource in most of the world, it seems inevitable that its icebergs will sooner or later be tapped, raising serious but not insurmountable legal, ecological and climatic questions and uncertainties.

Disposal of radioactive wastes, now prohibited by the Antarctic

Treaty, might some day become an attractive proposition, especially for crowded industrial countries. Opposition would of course be vehement, and amending the treaty would be difficult, perhaps impossible. But as nuclear wastes mount and as factions fight over disposal sites and the effectiveness of disposal technology, the idea of an international burying ground in the Transantarctic Mountains might become appealing. The initial cost would be high, but sharing might make it manageable, and the costs of maintenance and security might be relatively low.

Alternative energy sources are potentially available and could unquestionably be developed, but only for local consumption. There are more than a dozen volcanoes in Antarctica that might be tapped for geothermal energy. The strong and fairly steady winds that plunge toward the coast from the high interior have long been seen as a possible source of energy for light and heat and for conversion to hydrogen as a fuel for transportation. But in addition to some serious technological problems, neither prospect has appeared economic. The alternative energy source most likely to be developed soon is solar power, which might be usefully harnessed during those months when the sun never sets and scientific stations are most active. (The Americans tried using nuclear energy at the base in McMurdo Sound in the 1960s. It proved to be startlingly inefficient and very nearly disastrous: the reactor leaked and had to be removed in pieces for burial in the United States, along with thousands of tons of radioactive earth and gravel.)

Transportation and communication were expected to be among the continent's principal uses, but the development of long-range jet planes destroyed the idea that Antarctica would serve as a hub of intercontinental air traffic; and communication satellites have overtaken the notion that Antarctica would be the site of major relay stations for radio transmission.

Cold storage of meat and grain in the natural, energy-free deep freeze of Antarctica seemed an attractive idea to early pioneers, but the enormous round-trip distances involved, plus more-efficient methods of freezing, now make the proposition remote.

4

'The Interest of All Mankind'

These words enshrined in the Antarctic Treaty have repeatedly been used by the Consultative Parties both to acknowledge an obligation to the global community and to convey the impression that they were indeed meeting their responsibilities as trustees. The rest of the world was understandably skeptical and recently has expressed its dissatisfaction in the UN. The notion that a handful of mostly rich nations should have the exclusive power to make decisions possibly affecting everyone has increasingly been seen as unacceptable.

In December 1947 when the UN was young, almost universally admired, and about a third of its present size, a proposal was made in the Trusteeship Council that the polar regions, North and South, should be placed under the aegis of the UN. There was considerable support for the idea as it applied to Antarctica. However, linking the suggestion with the Arctic was a mistake, for across that frozen sea the Eastern and Western blocs were already glaring at each other in fear and hostility. Liberal intellectual opinion, especially in the English-speaking world, continued to favor UN sovereignty in Antarctica. But of the 12 nations that would conduct scientific research there during the IGY and subsequently negotiate the Antarctic Treaty, only New Zealand publicly supported the creation of a "world territory" under UN trusteeship.

In 1956, as the IGY was beginning to focus attention on the South Polar region, India requested that "The Question of Antarctica" be inscribed on the agenda of the next General Assembly. In the face of considerable opposition, especially from Chile and Argentina, the proposal was withdrawn, but was renewed two years later in more palatable form. However, by then plans for the Antarctic Treaty Conference were already under way, and again India was persuaded to withdraw its request.

Thereafter, Antarctica was rarely mentioned in the UN until this decade. In 1971 the question arose whether a UN survey of global resources should include estimates for Antarctica (the answer proved negative), and from 1974 onward the Food and Agriculture Organization (FAO) of the UN discussed Antarctic krill and related matters. In 1975, the United Nations Environment Program (UNEP) tried to involve itself in establishing ecologically sound guidelines for the exploration and exploitation of Antarctic resources, but was deterred by the treaty's Consultative Parties from adding this issue to its already overcrowded agenda.

The subject of Antarctica was raised in the General Assembly for the first time by Shirley Amerasinghe of Sri Lanka, who was soon to become president of the 1976 General Assembly. He offered no specific proposal, but his message was clear: the UN should involve itself in Antarctica, especially to uphold "the principle of equitable sharing of the world's resources." At the time, only Peru joined Sri Lanka in articulating the proper responsibility of the UN in Antarctica.

Ambassador Amerasinghe said he hoped his remarks would not "create a flutter in any dovecotes," but of course they did, and for two particular reasons. He was one of the most respected spokesmen of the Third World, and he was at the time president of the Law of the Sea (LOS) Conference, the long-playing

National Science Foundation photo by Russ Kinne
Two scientists collect rock samples in an ice-free valley of southern Victoria Land.

negotiation that the United States did much to initiate and ultimately rejected. During a decade of talks, Antarctica was often in the delegates' minds, though by unwritten agreement the subject was tabu until a Convention on the Law of the Sea could be achieved. Chile and Argentina were, of course, members of the so-called Group of 77, representing the less-developed countries and by now numbering well over a hundred. These two Consultative Parties, among the original drafters of the Antarctic Treaty, made it clear to their Third World colleagues that Antarctica was an unmentionable subject; if pressed, it would destroy the LOS Conference.

Law of the Sea

The LOS Conference appeared to impinge on Antarctica in two particular respects. Many UN members asked, if after decades of controversy sovereignty in Antarctica has not been established, should not Antarctica be considered "the common heritage of mankind" like the floor of the sea? If territorial claims are in conflict and go unrecognized by both superpowers, how can the common heritage principle be denied? If most of the nonclaimant nations recognize UN authority over areas of the seabed outside national jurisdiction, and if they assert that no national jurisdiction exists in Antarctica, how can they question the right of the international seabed authority to claim responsibility for Antarctic resources outward from the shoreline? When the United States refused to adopt the convention, delayed its completion by an additional year, and finally refused to sign, the Third World was even less disposed to accept the legitimacy of the Antarctic Treaty system.

The LOS Conference revealed that the concept of common heritage embraced by the Third World differed from that of most developed countries, certainly the United States. The latter interpreted the common heritage as virtually synonymous with "the commons," defined by the deputy head of the U.S. delegation as "those areas beyond the jurisdiction of any state which are available for the use of all." This was consistent with the policy of "open access," long insisted upon by the United States in Antarctica. But to the less-developed countries, this seemed a cover for the rich and powerful to exploit resources, whether on the seabed or in Antarctica, that less technologically advanced nations could not reach. In their perception, the common heritage belonged to all in equal shares.

The second area of sensitivity created by the LOS Conference, and later formalized in the convention, was its decision to grant coastal states living and mineral marine resources up to 200 miles from their shores. In Antarctica, the claiming of these so-called exclusive economic zones (EEZs) would complicate the claims issue even further. To avoid the appearance of defaulting on their declared rights, the claimant states must assert their sovereignty over their Antarctic EEZs. But this can be interpreted as an enlargement of claims, hence a violation of the Antarctic Treaty. The claimant states have gone through a variety of legal convolutions in an effort to escape this dilemma.

As had been anticipated, as soon as a Convention on the Law of the Sea was finally adopted, global attention turned to Antarctica. The issue was raised in the 1982 General Assembly by Malaysia and was discussed further at a meeting of the Nonaligned Movement in New Delhi the following spring. Confident of broad support, Malaysia, together with Antigua and Barbuda, was successful in placing the issue on the agenda of the 1983 General Assembly. In the subsequent debate, Third World spokesmen swung between acknowledging some merit in the Antarctic Treaty system and demanding a share in decisionmaking; between declaring that the treaty should be preserved and condemning it for creating an exclusive club. A compromise resolution was adopted by consensus, calling on the secretary-general "to prepare a comprehensive, factual and objective study on all aspects of Antarctica, taking fully into account the Antarctic Treaty system and other relevant factors." When the report came up for discussion in the General Assembly a year later (November 1984), the debate was lackluster and inconclusive, in part because the Consultative Parties by then had blunted some of the principal objections to the treaty system.

Objections and Responses

Why, members of the Group of 77 asked, should Antarctica fall under the jurisdiction of a handful of self-appointed nations? The region is patently of international concern, while the treaty system is exclusive, secretive, unaccountable and intrinsically unfair, they said. The rights and roles of states acceding to the treaty (but not accepted as Consultative Parties) are obscure or negligible, and there is no incentive to become parties to a treaty from which the majority is excluded from playing any responsible part. What the "club members" call their "special responsibility" has never been defined and provides no assurance that resources will be equitably shared. Especially galling is the consultative membership of South Africa, a country repeatedly condemned in the UN for its racial policies. Its participation in decisionmaking on behalf of "all mankind" in Antarctica is insupportable. Finally, the common-heritage concept is entirely appropriate and applicable to Antarctica. So, in general, speak those excluded from consultative status in Antarctica.

The response of the Consultative Parties has been twofold. On the one hand, they invited two of the largest Third World countries, India and Brazil, to join the club and subsequently accepted China and Uruguay. This can be read either as the natural consequence of these nations' demonstrated scientific interest in Antarctica or as a successful co-opting of the most influential members of the Group of 77. Further, the Consultative Parties invited states acceding to the Antarctic Treaty to send observers to their negotiations on a minerals regime and to attend their biennial meetings as nonvoting participants in both plenary and committee meetings, with the right to speak, receive all documentation, and offer written submissions. They also opened their doors to a greater number of UN agencies, international organizations and nongovernmental organizations (although this is still under negotiation). And they made progress in releasing a great deal more documentation than had previously been available.

These indications of flexibility and responsiveness were offset by the other aspect of the Consultative Parties' strategy. When it came to yielding authority or granting the UN a role, they dug in their heels. They successfully opposed the creation of a UN Committee on Antarctica "to promote and facilitate detailed discussion of specific issues." They insisted that the Antarctic Treaty system was not a closed system but was open to all with demonstrated interest. They declined to discuss more-formal measures of accountability than those already existing. And they contended that if there were shortcomings in the treaty system, these would be resolved within the system, which had repeatedly demonstrated its flexibility and the responsibility of its members.

U.S. Navy photo by Dana Babin

The main building at the U.S. Palmer Station on the Antarctic Peninsula

A spectacular event in January 1985 may have eased tensions—possibly even differences—between those within and outside the Antarctic Treaty system. The United States flew 57 individuals from 25 countries to the South Pole and six days of informal, off-the-record talks at the newly built Beardmore Camp 5,000 feet up in Antarctica's Transantarctic Mountains. In the group were journalists, lawyers, scientists, environmentalists and diplomats, including the Third World's chief spokesman on Antarctica, the Malaysian ambassador to the UN. The initiative for the meeting was taken by a group of individuals, and formal sponsorship resided in the Polar Research Board of the National Academy of Sciences. The cost, in the neighborhood of $1 million, was borne by the National Science Foundation and a group of private foundations. Significantly, individuals from 21 nontreaty states were invited and only 6 accepted, giving plausibility to the contention of the Consultative Parties that most nations are not seriously interested in Antarctica.

Some observers believe that discord over the future of Antarctica has already peaked, others that the issue will build toward 1991, when the treaty may come up for review. Certainly the developing countries have been through an educative process in recent years and have shed some illusions. Just as they learned that the seabed was not a source of instant wealth, they now have a far greater appreciation of the remoteness of resource exploitation in Antarctica. They have shown a grudging respect for the treaty system and are more inclined to acknowledge that it has served the global community well by keeping part of the world demilitarized and promoting cooperation among nations with deep antagonisms. Finally, they recognize that for the most part the Consultative Parties have behaved responsibly if arbitrarily. Although none of this has necessarily altered their conviction that Antarctica should be treated as the common heritage of mankind or that the UN should be involved, it may have tempered their criticisms.

The Environmentalists

Primarily because of their intense concern for the great whales, environmentalists have long had an interest in Antarctica, and they have had some influence on policy—at least among the English-speaking treaty countries. And because they are so often critics of the Consultative Parties, environmental organizations sometimes appear to be allies of the Third World, sharing similar views and objectives. This is probably inaccurate. The conservation community is by no means agreed on how the Antarctic environment can best be protected and is not sure that the UN would be a more responsible and responsive guardian of the environment than the Consultative Parties. It is assumed that the developing countries are generally more interested in resource exploitation than in conservation.

In the same year that the United Nations Environment Program was created, 1972, the Second World Conference on National Parks adopted a resolution urging that Antarctica be made a world park under the aegis of the UN. This idea is still vigorously promoted, although the World National Parks Congress in late 1982 adopted a more cautious recommendation, asking only that Antarctica be given "an internationally protected area designation which connotes worldwide its unique character and values...." The International Union for Conservation of Nature and Natural Resources (IUCN), at its general assembly in November 1984, similarly refrained from asking for the whole loaf. Presumably its members understand that it is unrealistic to hope that all of Antarctica will be set aside as a world park, immune in perpetuity from any kind of development.

Public Scrutiny?

With some justification, most environmentalists are skeptical that the Consultative Parties are faithfully adhering to the high standards that they have set down on paper. As a case in point, they cite a French airfield on the Adélie Coast, begun without an adequate environmental impact assessment as urged in the Consultative Parties' own rules. Environmentalists have forced two assessments, but believe that adequate procedures for evaluating the impact of future projects are still lacking. Among other objectives, they want public scrutiny of Antarctic operations to ensure that environmental protection measures are being observed. One suggestion is to create an independent Antarctic Environment Protection Agency to carry out review, assessment, monitoring and inspection functions. Conservationists would like to see more and larger areas set aside as permanent preserves and a moratorium on resource development until protection of the environment can be absolutely assured. They are also concerned that a proliferation of scientific stations, almost always on Antarctica's coasts, will dangerously pollute and otherwise disturb the marine environment and the limited ice-free areas.

At their 12th meeting, the Consultative Parties responded with two recommendations on the environment. The first urged that they reexamine how their activities affect the environment and asked the Scientific Committee on Antarctic Research to elaborate specific procedures for impact assessment. The second proposed that the Consultative Parties update the code of conduct for disposal of wastes, taking advantage of improved technologies. These topics were discussed further at the 13th meeting in Brussels in October 1985.

5

The Future of the Treaty System

Contrary to the perception of many, the Antarctic Treaty system is evolving rapidly, overcoming the charge of exclusivity by expanding to include nearly 3 billion of the world's 4 billion people. That is, with the addition of China and Uruguay to the Consultative Parties, three quarters of the world's people are now represented in the governing body of Antarctica. The remainder are not excluded, but may participate in deliberations if they have acceded to the treaty. It can hardly be said any longer that Antarctica is controlled by an exclusive club. If it is galling to some that this proven system exists outside the UN and remains unaccountable to it, they might consider well the reasons.

The Consultative Parties have not permitted irrelevant disputes to distract them from their purpose. They have exploited common interests instead of differences and managed to overlook their sharp antagonisms. In recent years, two of the parties have been in a bitter war (Britain and Argentina over the Falkland [Malvinas] Islands). Two others (Chile and Argentina) have several times been on the verge of war over the long-disputed islands in the Beagle Channel at the tip of South America—a dispute only recently settled. Moreover, both these fights were seen by the participants to bear on the issue of conflicting claims in Antarctica. Yet hostilities did not spread south of the 60th parallel; indeed discussion on Antarctic matters remained civil at all times, in part no doubt because meetings were conducted in private and no nationalistic posing was required. To continue the catalogue of tensions, one party (South Africa) is in varying degrees anathema to all others. In other forums, the hostility between the United States and the Soviet Union often dominates debate. Yet, for a quarter of a century, the Antarctic Treaty system has somehow worked. Why then, many ask, try to fix it?

One of the arguments against passing responsibility for Antarctica to the UN has been that 12 or even 18 experienced and concerned nations can perform more efficiently than 150 and more. Now as the number of contracting states grows—both those with consultative status and those without—concern must be felt about the continuing ability of the parties to act with dispatch. When it becomes clear that the UN cannot force the issue, that the Antarctic Treaty system will survive unchanged in its essentials, many more nations may find it desirable to accede to the treaty. When all have the right to be heard, will the biennial meetings of the Consultative Parties begin to resemble the UN General Assembly? And will the pressure for consultative status increase the number of decisionmakers to the point where consensus becomes impossible to achieve, or so time-consuming that important issues are allowed to drift? And when there are more participants and more publicity, will it still be possible for the Consultative Parties to ignore their fundamental differences beyond Antarctica? These are disturbing questions, which must qualify one's enthusiasm for the efforts of the Consultative Parties to make the Antarctic Treaty system more responsive to the world community.

There is another danger posed by the perceived advantages of achieving consultative status. Traditionally, the method of establishing qualifications for admission to the inner circle has been to build a scientific station, almost invariably on the coast, where access is most convenient. A disproportionate number of these

National Science Foundation
photo by Russ Kinne

Scott tents used by researchers working in the field in northern Victoria Land.

bases have been built on the Antarctic Peninsula where claims are overlapping, the climate is less savage and the darkness of winter less prolonged. Each adds to the burden on Antarctica's fragile ecosystems. It would be desirable for nations with established scientific programs to invite those nations newly interested in Antarctica to share existing facilities, where possible on a cost-sharing basis. There is well-established precedent, for ever since the IGY, scientists from a wide range of nations have been invited to spend a season on the ice. In a recent year, 47 foreign scientists from 17 countries worked at U.S. stations. What is needed now is to expand on these collaborative efforts by making clear that newcomers can attain consultative status without establishing national stations. This might also reduce the danger that developing nations may spend extravagantly in Antarctica merely to achieve the prestige associated with consultative status.

Indeed, there are a variety of arguments for defining more clearly what constitutes qualifications for election to consultative status. All the treaty says is that a state must demonstrate "its interest in Antarctica by conducting substantial scientific research activity there, such as the establishment of a scientific station or the dispatch of a scientific expedition." Whatever this means precisely, the original signatories of the treaty are exempt from it. Belgium has conducted no research in Antarctica for years; Norway takes part only occasionally and on a very small scale. Is this fair? Many nations think not. On the other hand, the pioneering role of these countries should stand for something, and their calm and disinterested voices have value at meetings of the treaty nations.

There is a positive side to the enlargement of the decisionmaking body for Antarctica, beyond making it more democratic. It seems possible that, as the number of Consultative Parties grows and the claimant nations thereby become an ever smaller minority, the claims issue may be moderated or become eroded. Such expectations have been disappointed in the past, however; in 1959 it was widely expected that the Antarctic Treaty itself would have this effect—an unfulfilled hope.

One of the most positive recent developments is the growing interest among developing countries in Antarctic science. As it has become more apparent that profits from Antarctic resources are not imminent, appreciation of the possible benefits of science in Antarctica has grown. Some developing nations are now focusing less on how they can change the political machinery of Antarctica and more on how they can tap into scientific knowledge acquired there. Under the terms of the Antarctic Treaty, this knowledge must be shared, but in practice it is not easily accessible and there is always some suspicion, even among the Consultative Parties, that information is being withheld. The invariable answer of the accused (generally the Soviet Union) is that raw data is useless and processing takes time and money. It will be even more difficult for the Consultative Parties to process and select data that will be of particular value to scientists of the Third World, but the effort may be well worth it.

The hope that Antarctica might be treated as the common heritage of mankind is no longer an attainable goal. Unlike the seabed or outer space, Antarctica has too much history, too long a record of human activity, too firm a body of international law not easily overturned. The concept of the common heritage simply cannot be reconciled with the Antarctic Treaty, which thus far remains a rare example of man's capacity for international cooperation. It is neither desirable nor feasible to put something else in its place. The threat that, if the Consultative Parties are obstinate, the UN will establish a parallel system is quite improbable, for all the outsiders together lack the resources, the organization, the science and technology to become effective in Antarctica.

In any test of strength, the nontreaty nations are faced with a formidable opponent, against whom they have very modest leverage. For the Consultative Parties to the Antarctic Treaty represent the largest, most powerful aggregation of nations that has ever operated consensually within a legal framework to fulfill specific purposes. As long as they act together with a modicum of rationality, any other alignment of nations will be impotent. The danger to the treaty does not come from without, from the UN, but from the possibility that Antarctica will lose its immunity from the divisive issues that elsewhere make angry adversaries of the treaty members. Preservation of the Antarctic Treaty system does not ensure that this danger will be avoided, but it offers the best hope.

Talking It Over

A Note for Students and Discussion Groups

This issue of the HEADLINE SERIES, like its predecessors, is published for every serious reader, specialized or not, who takes an interest in the subject. Many of our readers will be in classrooms, seminars or community discussion groups. Particularly with them in mind, we present below some discussion questions—suggested as a starting point only—and references for further reading.

Discussion Questions

What are the principal resources of Antarctica? Do you believe they will ever be exploited on a significant scale? What are the major obstacles to the development of Antarctic resources?

Which nations have asserted territorial claims in Antarctica? Why has the United States refrained from making a claim? Do you think the United States ought to have staked a claim when other nations were doing so?

What are the most important provisions of the Antarctic Treaty? What are the two or three things about it that are most remarkable? What has made it possible for the treaty to evolve? Do you believe the Consultative Parties have behaved responsibly?

The author suggests at least eight ways in which science has played an important role in Antarctica. How many can you name? Do you believe Antarctica should be preserved entirely for science?

In your opinion, is the concept of the common heritage of mankind appropriate to Antarctica? What are the obstacles? What are the principal arguments of those opposed to the present governance of Antarctica? Do you agree with the author's conclusion that it is neither desirable nor feasible to replace the treaty system?

READING LIST

Chapman, Walter [Robert Silverberg], *The Loneliest Continent*. Greenwich, Conn., New York Graphic Society Publishers, 1964. A well-balanced popular history.

Dugger, John A., "Exploiting Antarctic Mineral Resources—Technology, Economics, and the Environment," *University of Miami Law Review*, December 1978. Possibly the most useful article in an issue devoted to Antarctica.

Kirwan, L. P., *A History of Polar Exploration*. New York, W.W. Norton, 1960. A standard British work by the then director of the Royal Geographical Society; an excellent survey.

McWhinnie, Mary A., and Denys, Charlene J., "The High Importance of the Lowly Krill," *Natural History*, March 1980. Two of the most knowledgable marine biologists provide the essentials of the subject in a readable article.

Polar Regions Atlas. Washington, D.C., Central Intelligence Agency, 1978. Besides excellent maps, this short work provides a great deal of hard information about Antarctica.

Proceedings of the Workshop on the Antarctic Treaty System, 7-13 January 1985, Transantarctic Mountains, Antarctica. Washington, D.C., Polar Research Board, National Academy of Sciences, 1985. This conference, mentioned in the text, produced papers representing a wide range of political viewpoints.

Quigg, Philip W., *A Pole Apart: The Emerging Issue of Antarctica*. A Twentieth Century Fund Report. New York, McGraw-Hill, 1983. The only comprehensive treatment of Antarctica: history, politics, economics, science and technology.

Shackleton, Sir Ernest H., *South: The Story of Shackleton's Last Expedition, 1914-17*. New York, Macmillan, 1920. One of the greatest Antarctic explorers coolly narrates one of the continent's most harrowing sagas.

Sullivan, Walter, *Quest for a Continent*. New York, McGraw-Hill, 1957. Especially good on early science and the later Byrd expeditions, in one of which the author participated.

Vicuna, F. Orrego, ed., *Antarctic Resources Policy: Scientific, Legal, and Political Issues*. London, Cambridge University Press, 1983. A collection of highly authoritative papers from the first international conference ever held in Antarctica.

Wright, N.A., and Williams, P.L., eds., *Mineral Resources of Antarctica*. Reston, Va., U.S. Geological Survey, 1974. As a basic source, this short work has not been superseded.

Zumberge, James H., ed., *Possible Environmental Effects of Mineral Exploration and Exploitation in Antarctica*. Cambridge, England, Scientific Committee on Antarctic Research, 1979. The chairman of SCAR pulls together the assessments of experts in many fields.

The Antarctic Treaty

Signed at Washington December 1, 1959
Ratification advised by U.S. Senate August 10, 1960
Ratified by U.S. President August 18, 1960
U.S. ratification deposited at Washington August 18, 1960
Proclaimed by U.S. President June 23, 1961
Entered into force June 23, 1961

The Governments of Argentina, Australia, Belgium, Chile, the French Republic, Japan, New Zealand, Norway, the Union of South Africa, the Union of Soviet Socialist Republics, the United Kingdom of Great Britain and Northern Ireland, and the United States of America,

Recognizing that it is in the interest of all mankind that Antarctica shall continue forever to be used exclusively for peaceful purposes and shall not become the scene or object of international discord;

Acknowledging the substantial contributions to scientific knowledge resulting from international cooperation in scientific investigation in Antarctica;

Convinced that the establishment of a firm foundation for the continuation and development of such cooperation on the basis of freedom of scientific investigation in Antarctica as applied during the International Geophysical Year accords with the interests of science and the progress of all mankind;

Convinced also that a treaty ensuring the use of Antarctica for peaceful purposes only and the continuance of international harmony in Antarctica will further the purposes and principles embodied in the Charter of the United Nations;

Have agreed as follows:

Article I

1. Antarctica shall be used for peaceful purposes only. There shall be prohibited, *inter alia*, any measures of a military nature, such as the establishment of military bases and fortifications, the carrying out of military maneuvers, as well as the testing of any type of weapons.

2. The present Treaty shall not prevent the use of military personnel or equipment for scientific research or for any other peaceful purposes.

Article II

Freedom of scientific investigation in Antarctica and cooperation toward that end, as applied during the International Geophysical Year, shall continue, subject to the provisions of the present Treaty.

Article III

1. In order to promote international cooperation in scientific investigation in Antarctica, as provided for in Article II of the present Treaty, the Contracting Parties agree that, to the greatest extent feasible and practicable:
    (a) information regarding plans for scientific programs in Antarctica shall be exchanged to permit maximum economy and efficiency of operations;
    (b) scientific personnel shall be exchanged in Antarctica between expeditions and stations;
    (c) scientific observations and results from Antarctica shall be exchanged and made freely available.
2. In implementing this Article, every encouragement shall be given to the establishment of cooperative working relations with those Specialized Agencies of the United Nations and other international organizations having a scientific or technical interest in Antarctica.

Article IV

1. Nothing contained in the present Treaty shall be interpreted as:
    (a) a renunciation by any Contracting Party of previously asserted rights of or claims to territorial sovereignty in Antarctica;
    (b) a renunciation or diminution by any Contracting Party of any basis of claim to territorial sovereignty in Antarctica which it may have whether as a result of its activities or those of its nationals in Antarctica, or otherwise;
    (c) prejudicing the position of any Contracting Party as regards its recognition or non-recognition of any other State's right of or claim or basis of claim to territorial sovereignty in Antarctica.
2. No acts or activities taking place while the present Treaty is in force shall constitute a basis for asserting, supporting or denying a claim to territorial sovereignty in Antarctica or create any rights of sovereignty in Antarctica. No new claim, or enlargement of an existing claim, to territorial sovereignty in Antarctica shall be asserted while the present Treaty is in force.

Article V

1. Any nuclear explosions in Antarctica and the disposal there of radioactive waste material shall be prohibited.
2. In the event of the conclusion of international agreements concerning the use of nuclear energy, including nuclear explosions and the disposal of radioactive waste material, to which all of the Contracting Parties whose representatives are entitled to participate in the meetings provided for under Article IX are parties, the rules established under such agreements shall apply in Antarctica.

Article VI

The provisions of the present Treaty shall apply to the area south of 60° South Latitude, including all ice shelves, but nothing in the present Treaty shall prejudice or in any way affect the rights, or the exercise of the rights, of any State under international law with regard to the high seas within that area.

Article VII

1. In order to promote the objectives and ensure the observance of the provisions of the present Treaty, each Contracting Party whose representatives are entitled to participate in the meetings referred to in Article IX of the Treaty shall have the right to designate observers to carry out any inspection provided for by the present Article. Observers shall be nationals of the Contracting Parties which designate them. The names of observers shall be communicated to every other Contracting Party having the right to designate observers, and like notice shall be given of the termination of their appointment.

2. Each observer designated in accordance with the provisions of paragraph 1 of this Article shall have complete freedom of access at any time to any or all areas of Antarctica.

3. All areas of Antarctica, including all stations, installations and equipment within those areas, and all ships and aircraft at points of discharging or embarking cargoes or personnel in Antarctica, shall be open at all times to inspection by any observers designated in accordance with paragraph 1 of this Article.

4. Aerial observation may be carried out at any time over any or all areas of Antarctica by any of the Contracting Parties having the right to designate observers.

5. Each Contracting Party shall, at the time when the present Treaty enters into force for it, inform the other Contracting Parties, and thereafter shall give them notice in advance, of

   (a) all expeditions to and within Antarctica, on the part of its ships or nationals, and all expeditions to Antarctica organized in or proceeding from its territory;

   (b) all stations in Antarctica occupied by its nationals; and

   (c) any military personnel or equipment intended to be introduced by it into Antarctica subject to the conditions prescribed in paragraph 2 of Article I of the present Treaty.

Article VIII

1. In order to facilitate the exercise of their functions under the present Treaty, and without prejudice to the respective positions of the Contracting Parties relating to jurisdiction over all other persons in Antarctica, observers designated under paragraph 1 of Article VII and scientific personnel exchanged under subparagraph 1(b) of Article III of the Treaty, and members of the staffs accompanying any such persons, shall be subject only to the jurisdiction of the Contracting Party of which they are nationals in respect of all acts or omissions occurring while they are in Antarctica for the purpose of exercising their functions.

2. Without prejudice to the provisions of paragraph 1 of this Article, and pending the adoption of measures in pursuance of subparagraph 1(e) of Article IX, the Contracting Parties concerned in any case of dispute with regard to the exercise of jurisdiction in Antarctica shall immediately consult together with a view to reaching a mutually acceptable solution.

Article IX

1. Representatives of the Contracting Parties named in the preamble to the present Treaty shall meet at the City of Canberra within two months after the date of entry into

force of the Treaty, and thereafter at suitable intervals and places, for the purpose of exchanging information, consulting together on matters of common interest pertaining to Antarctica, and formulating and considering, and recommending to their Governments, measures in furtherance of the principles and objectives of the Treaty, including measures regarding:

(a) use of Antarctica for peaceful purposes only;
(b) facilitation of scientific research in Antarctica;
(c) facilitation of international scientific cooperation in Antarctica;
(d) facilitation of the exercise of the rights of inspection provided for in Article VII of the Treaty;
(e) questions relating to the exercise of jurisdiction in Antarctica;
(f) preservation and conservation of living resources in Antarctica.

2. Each Contracting Party which has become a party to the present Treaty by accession under Article XIII shall be entitled to appoint representatives to participate in the meetings referred to in paragraph 1 of the present Article, during such time as that Contracting Party demonstrates its interest in Antarctica by conducting substantial scientific research activity there, such as the establishment of a scientific station or the despatch of a scientific expedition.

3. Reports from the observers referred to in Article VII of the present Treaty shall be transmitted to the representatives of the Contracting Parties participating in the meetings referred to in paragraph 1 of the present Article.

4. The measures referred to in paragraph 1 of this Article shall become effective when approved by all the Contracting Parties whose representatives were entitled to participate in the meetings held to consider those measures.

5. Any or all of the rights established in the present Treaty may be exercised as from the date of entry into force of the Treaty whether or not any measures facilitating the exercise of such rights have been proposed, considered or approved as provided in this Article.

Article X

Each of the Contracting Parties undertakes to exert appropriate efforts, consistent with the Charter of the United Nations, to the end that no one engages in any activity in Antarctica contrary to the principles or purposes of the present Treaty.

Article XI

1. If any dispute arises between two or more of the Contracting Parties concerning the interpretation or application of the present Treaty, those Contracting Parties shall consult among themselves with a view to having the dispute resolved by negotiation, inquiry, mediation, conciliation, arbitration, judicial settlement or other peaceful means of their own choice.

2. Any dispute of this character not so resolved shall, with the consent, in each case, of all parties to the dispute, be referred to the International Court of Justice for settlement; but failure to reach agreement on reference to the International Court shall not absolve parties to the dispute from the responsibility of continuing to seek to resolve it by any of the various peaceful means referred to in paragraph 1 of this Article.

Article XII

1. (a) The present Treaty may be modified or amended at any time by unanimous agreement of the Contracting Parties whose representatives are entitled to participate in the meetings provided for under Article IX. Any such modification or amendment shall enter into force when the depositary Government has received notice from all such Contracting Parties that they have ratified it.

(b) Such modification or amendment shall thereafter enter into force as to any other Contracting Party when notice of ratification by it has been received by the depositary Government. Any such Contracting Party from which no notice of ratification is received within a period of two years from the date of entry into force of the modification or amendment in accordance with the provisions of subparagraph 1(a) of this Article shall be deemed to have withdrawn from the present Treaty on the date of the expiration of such period.

2. (a) If after the expiration of thirty years from the date of entry into force of the present Treaty, any of the Contracting Parties whose representatives are entitled to participate in the meetings provided for under Article IX so requests by a communication addressed to the depositary Government, a Conference of all the Contracting Parties shall be held as soon as practicable to review the operation of the Treaty.

(b) Any modification or amendment to the present Treaty which is approved at such a Conference by a majority of the Contracting Parties there represented, including a majority of those whose representatives are entitled to participate in the meetings provided for under Article IX, shall be communicated by the depositary Government to all the Contracting Parties immediately after the termination of the Conference and shall enter into force in accordance with the provisions of paragraph 1 of the present Article.

(c) If any such modification or amendment has not entered into force in accordance with the provisions of subparagraph 1(a) of this Article within a period of two years after the date of its communication to all the Contracting Parties, any Contracting Party may at any time after the expiration of that period give notice to the depositary Government of its withdrawal from the present Treaty; and such withdrawal shall take effect two years after the receipt of the notice of the depositary Government.

Article XIII

1. The present Treaty shall be subject to ratification by the signatory States. It shall be open for accession by any State which is a Member of the United Nations, or by any other State which may be invited to accede to the Treaty with the consent of all the Contracting Parties whose representatives are entitled to participate in the meetings provided for under Article IX of the Treaty.

2. Ratification of or accession to the present Treaty shall be effected by each State in accordance with its constitutional processes.

3. Instruments of ratification and instruments of accession shall be deposited with the Government of the United States of America, hereby designated as the depositary Government.

4. The depositary Government shall inform all signatory and acceding States of the date of each deposit of an instrument of ratification or accession, and the date of entry into force of the Treaty and of any modification or amendment thereto.

5. Upon the deposit of instruments of ratification by all the signatory States, the present

Treaty shall enter into force for those States and for States which have deposited instruments of accession. Thereafter the Treaty shall enter into force for any acceding State upon the deposit of its instrument of accession.

6. The present Treaty shall be registered by the depositary Government pursuant to Article 102 of the Charter of the United Nations.

Article XIV

The present Treaty, done in the English, French, Russian and Spanish languages, each version being equally authentic, shall be deposited in the archives of the Government of the United States of America, which shall transmit duly certified copies thereof to the Governments of the signatory and acceding States.

IN WITNESS WHEREOF the undersigned Plenipotentiaries, duly authorized, have signed the present Treaty.

DONE at Washington this first day of December, one thousand nine hundred and fifty-nine.

Text of the Antarctic Treaty from the 1982 edition of Arms Control and Disarmament Agreements *published by the United States Arms Control and Disarmament Agency.*

Antarctic Treaty

Contracting States

	Consultative Parties	Acceding Parties

original signatories {
- Argentina ⎫
- Australia ⎪
- Britain ⎪
- Chile ⎬ claimant states
- France ⎪
- New Zealand ⎪
- Norway ⎭
- Belgium
- Japan
- South Africa
- Soviet Union
- United States

- Poland (1977)
- West Germany (1981)
- Brazil (1983)
- India (1983)
- China (1985)
- Uruguay (1985)

Acceding Parties
- Czechoslovakia (1962)
- Denmark (1965)
- The Netherlands (1967)
- Rumania (1971)
- East Germany (1974)
- Bulgaria (1978)
- Peru (1981)
- Italy (1981)
- Papua New Guinea (1981)
- Spain (1982)
- Hungary (1984)
- Sweden (1984)
- Finland (1984)
- Cuba (1984)